© 2013
ISBN 1482704226

Published by Creative Combinations LLC
Text Copyright © 2012 C.G. Meloy
Illustration Copyright © 2012 Zachary Pullen

First Edition
'Life & Spectrum'
Book Design by Lindsey Grant
Meloy, C.G.
Life & Specturm / written by C.G. Meloy
Illustrated by Zachary Pullen

For inquiries, please visit:
www.lifeandspectrum.com

LIFE

&

SPECTRUM

A REVEALING LOOK AT HIGH FUNCTIONING AUTISM AND ASPERGER'S SYNDROME

WRITTEN BY C.G. MELOY ILLUSTRATED BY Z. PULLEN

table of contents

6. FOREWORD

8. PREFACE

10. WAR OF THE WORLDS

12. DISORDER, DISABILITY OR DIFFERENCE?

14. THE MOM FACTOR

16. AUDITORY ISSUES

18. BRAIN OVERLOAD & LOSING TIME

20. CLUMSY

22. REPETITIVE BEHAVIOR

24. ATYPICAL EATING

26. KNOWLEDGE

28. AWARENESS

30. THE STEPFORD KIDS

32. MIDDLE SCHOOL SHOCK

34. MADMAN ACROSS THE MIDDLE SCHOOL

36. VISUAL LEARNING AND MEMORIZATION

38. 3 GENERAL STRATEGIES

40. SELF ACCOMMODATION

42. DEVELOPMENTALLY ACCELERATED

44. THE DANISH GAMBIT

46. THE NEGATIVITY LOOP

48. COMPLEXITY AND COMPETING FACTORS

50. "I KNOW YOU CAN DO THAT"

52. LOWERED EXPECTATIONS

54. AVOIDING THE COOKIE CUTTER

56. TO REVEAL OR NOT TO REVEAL

58. TO SPEAK OR NOT TO SPEAK

60. TO THINK OR NOT TO THINK

62. THE DIFFICULT COWORKER

64. BEWILDERED EMPLOYERS

66. RUNNING ON EMPTY

68. LIVING INDEPENDENTLY

70. THE APPEAL OF THE NUCLEAR OPTION

72. EMOTIONAL EQUILIBRIUM

74. ECONOMICS

76. 3,2,1, ZERO!

78. BIKE BOY

80. INTERNAL COMBUSTION

82. CREATING MY OWN COMFORT ZONE

84. RAIN MAN

86. THE EPHEMERAL NATURE OF CLOSE FRIENDSHIPS

88. FRANKLY, SCARLETT...

90. THE OTHER SIDE OF THE COIN

92. PANTS ON FIRE

94. KEEN PERCEPTION

96. BEING BLUNT

98. THE SPHINCTER PRINCIPLE

100. JEKYLL AND HYDE

102. THE UNFORGIVABLE CRIME OF HAVING A PULSE

104. THE THING ABOUT SELF ESTEEM

106. THE THING ABOUT NAME-CALLING

108. THE THING ABOUT BULLYING

110. A TALE OF TWO DENSITIES

112. THE HYPOTHETICAL QUESTION

114. THE OTHER HYPOTHETICAL QUESTION

116. ARE ASPIES SMARTER THAN NTs?

118. MEDS

120. WHAT ABOUT THERAPY NOW?

122. SQUARE PEG, ROUND HOLE

124. THE MAYTAG REPAIRMAN

126. A NOTE FOR OCCUPATIONAL THERAPY STUDENTS

128. AUTISTIC ALCHEMY

130. NOT EASILY

132. DIVERSITY

In reflecting back on my first years of practice as a pediatric occupational therapist, it was a period of acquiring vast amounts of knowledge, tenacity and patience. I considered myself an expert. After 15 years of experience in the field, I have discovered that expertise comes only through the light of being a dedicated learner; a student of life. This is where true success and clinical efficacy come from.

This book, filled with honest reflection and sincere disclosure, is for all who work with, love, or are involved with an individual on the tender spectrum known as Autism. From its idiosyncratic grammar to its candid snippets of life on the Autism spectrum, the author takes the reader into his poignant experiences and perspectives. As an occupational therapist, this book will undoubtedly be an important reference in both my career and personal life.

Suzanna Morrison, MSOT, OTR/L

preface

this book is the result of the questions people ask me about my autism spectrum disorder. sometimes people with young family members on the autism spectrum are curious about my successes and failures. sometimes clinicians are interested in my ability to articulate my symptoms, strategies and experiences. because i have lived on the autism spectrum for a long time, i might know something that wasn't in their textbooks.

some of the things i write about are not designed to make me look good. there are some things i would rather keep private. but if this book is going to be worthwhile, then the content has to not only be true... but also revealing. dang it.

it is commonly thought that a majority of aspies do not work full-time. after decades in the workforce, i have developed a number of perspectives on employment that are insightful, perhaps even *incite*-ful.

i refer to normal people as "neurotypical", or "NTs". i refer to people with high functioning autism as "aspies". i use the word "normal" to mean in accordance with social norms.

this book is not intended to be an introduction to high functioning autism or asperger's syndrome. it is not academic. it is more like an informal case study. my comments are just my opinions. they happen to be correct, but they're just my opinions. this book is idiosyncratic and scattershot - just like my brain. ~

war of the worlds

there are two worlds in which i have to exist. the first is the childlike, solitary, autism world. the second is the adult, social, neurotypical world. i have to be in the first because of my nature, but i have to be in the second in order to function. walking the tightrope between two worlds is not easy. these worlds do not *meet*, they *collide*. autism may not be life threatening, but it can be *quality of life* threatening. ~

disorder, disability or difference?

yes. all of the above. high functioning autism is a disorder for me, because it significantly hinders my functionality in the neurotypical world. it is also a disability, because i don't have the ability to process non verbal cues well. but there is a sense in which it is just a difference. i have a different set of abilities and impairments. the only reason why it is a disorder is because of how the numbers break down. if 98% of people were on the autism spectrum, then the remaining 2% would be thought of as having a disorder. we might call it "hyper-social disorder", or maybe "social butterfly syndrome". being on the autism spectrum is not the issue. being on the autism spectrum *in the neurotypical world* is the issue. ~

the mom factor

sometimes a mother of an aspie son can be quite intrigued with me. she will recognize some of my behaviors. she wonders if i represent what her child will be like as an adult. she wants to know if her son will be able to drive a car and work a job... like me. she wants to know if her son will have a career, get married and be a parent... unlike me. in some ways she is hoping her child does as well as i have, yet in other ways she is hoping her child won't be as pathetic as i am! but i understand. i suggest that her child can do quite well, due to the benefits of having an early diagnosis, an individual education plan and various therapies. but there is another huge factor in the kid's success - MOM is looking out for him. ~

auditory issues

i hear sounds and voices that are not real. i've had these issues since childhood. they are distracting, confusing, annoying and troubling. i do not like them. they sound just as authentic as real sounds and real voices. my auditory issues are mild. episodes may only last for a minute or less. often i can quickly determine if they are real, by considering probability. if i'm alone, then i know a voice isn't real. if i hear a sound, i might look at other people in the room to ascertain if they are hearing it also. if no one else is reacting, then i know it's not real. i try to stay focused on whatever task is at hand, and i may seem tentative while it's happening. if it ever became constant, i don't know how i could continue to live in any productive way.

i've wondered if these pseudo-sounds that i hear are the result of my brain's inability to process certain data. i'm very sensitive to all kinds of environmental stimuli including smells, sounds, light and vibrations. perhaps my brain senses some of this data, but processes it into something else. sometimes i hear pseudo-sounds when there is a constant background noise. i might hear the pseudo-sound of a telephone ringing, along with the real sound of an air conditioner or an engine.

when i was young, the most disturbing auditory issue i had was that i would occasionally hear an electronic beeping sound that originated from inside my head. all of the other pseudo-sounds seemed to be external, so the beeping one was particularly troubling. it made me wonder if i was something less than human. sometimes other people would wonder the exact same thing about me. ~

Brain overload & losing time

when i have too much sensory input, my brain can't keep up. it can't process that much data - at least not in real time - especially with multifaceted stimuli. if someone suddenly moves toward me, touches me, makes eye contact with me and quickly asks me questions... my brain won't register everything that just happened, at least not in real time. if i do process everything, it might take a few seconds for my brain to catch up.

sometimes my perception will be like a science fiction movie where reality freezes, and then contracts and expands. it is very unsettling. it's like i'm in a snow globe, and someone has just shook me and my world. it's like i'm in a dream or another dimension. afterward i will have to find dark solitude as soon as i can.

if you've ever had a night terror where you were unsure if you were awake or still dreaming, then imagine an extreme, paralyzed version of that. consider the sensation you feel when you jump into a cold swimming pool. for a few seconds you might feel the shock of suddenly entering another world, before you acclimate. now suppose that such an encompassing sensation can overtake you when you are in a social setting, or a fast moving environment. now multiply the intensity by about thirteen million... - welcome to my world.

sometimes i don't experience the altered perception, and i simply lose time. it happens a lot in a minor way, and occasionally it happens in a more consequential way. if the duration is only about one second, then i might just continue with what i'm doing. but if it's a few seconds or more, then i may not be very functional for the rest of the day. my decisions about how i live my life may seem curious to others, but my choices are designed to help me avoid brain overload and losing time. it's not about thriving - it's about surviving. ~

clumsy

like many people on the autism spectrum, i am quite clumsy. it has been an ostracizing factor for me, because some social activities require physical coordination. sports teams, ice skating, roller skating, skateboarding, skiing and dancing were popular among my peers, but i couldn't excel at those activities. often i couldn't participate at all.

i am sometimes unaware that i have bumped into something. i frequently have scrapes or bruises that i don't know the source of. my knack at falling on stairs is legendary. unfortunately the humor is undeniable, because i mostly fell when i was going up the stairs, not down. people always thought that was so funny. it rarely happens now, because after 30 or 40 years i eventually learned to be careful. "developmentally delayed", indeed. ~

repetitive behavior

when i was young, i could ride my bike around in a circle for hours. i can still do that even now. the only difference is that now i understand that such behavior is not normal. sometimes i will listen to the same song over and over for hours, perhaps even all day. i don't get tired of it. i fully enjoy it each time, with no diminishing return. when i was young, there was a particular 8-track that i would play all day long. my family grew to hate it. they would throw it away, and i would dig it out of the trash. the tape would come out of the cartridge, and i would lovingly spool it back in. the halves of the cartridge would separate, and i would tape them back together. i never got sick of hearing it. i didn't understand how everyone else could tire of it.

sometimes i repeat certain numbers, words and sounds. i have no idea why. it doesn't seem to correlate with levels of stress or anxiety, nor is it related to any interest that i have. my best guess is that i do it because my brain is wired to do it. i might try to avoid doing it in public, but sometimes i'm not aware that i'm doing it. if there was any substantial meaning, i think i would have figured it out by now.

repetitive behavior seems very natural for me. sometimes repetitive activity seems to free my mind to think about whatever i want to think about. when i would play a video game or a pinball machine for hours, my mind would be deep in thought about something unrelated. i might do my best thinking when i'm walking, shooting baskets, or riding a bicycle around in a circle. sometimes i can be quite content doing something very simple. i don't spend all day staring at a tree, but i'm closer to being like that than anyone realizes. ~

atypical eating

i laughed out loud when i learned that odd eating habits were a symptom of autism. i once spent a summer eating only canned spaghetti. i once spent about six months eating only pizza. i won't eat anything unless it looks good and smells good. i'm wary of food with many ingredients. in my view, a complex dish is more likely to include something undesirable. i don't understand why people put coffee in brownies, raw eggs in salad dressing, cottage cheese in lasagna... -

there are many common foods that i have never tried including coffee, cottage cheese, pickles, and sour cream. smell and texture are very important to me. just the smell of buttermilk or parmesan can make me vomit. a strong coffee smell can give me a headache. i tend to like a crispy texture. soft, runny textures may not interest me. there is one food that i have never tried, that i am curious about. it doesn't pass the eye test, but it smells wonderful. chili. if i ever throw caution to the wind and get totally wild, i might try chili. it smells so good.

people were always amazed that i could tell the difference when they would try to trick me. someone tried putting cheap ketchup in the brand name bottle. i knew immediately that it wasn't right. someone made some plain ice tea once. i wouldn't drink it, because it smelled like mandarin spice tea. she had kept the two different types of tea bags in the same container, but didn't think anyone could possibly notice any transference. i didn't know that she had mandarin spice tea, but i remembered the scent from one of my food service jobs. people were always surprised that my senses were that discerning. ~

knowledge

my brain remembers a lot of knowledge, and much of it is useless. i have little or no control over what my brain elects to remember. it would be quite an asset if i could control it. memorization was a useful compensating skill that i had as a child, but i no longer have that ability. sometimes i certainly know the answer to a question, perhaps with stunning detail. but often when i am asked a question, my brain just puts forth an answer. i don't know if the answer is correct. i just know that's the answer that my brain is putting forward. fortunately, the answer my brain puts forward is almost always correct. ~

awareness

other people thought that i was an odd kid, but i didn't think i was odd. i was wrong about that. i'm still odd, but now i'm much more aware of it. as i progressed in elementary school i knew that i was different, but i didn't think about it too much unless i had to. my body was the only body i had ever lived in. my brain was the only brain i had ever had. my peculiarities were normal for me.

i would think about the auditory issues while they were happening, but afterward i would dismiss them and move on. on occasions when i would lose time, i was often in a situation where i could assume that it was because i had hit my head. i didn't know that it was my brain being overwhelmed with more sensory data than it could process. i was a late talker, but my family thought it was because i received so much attention that i didn't need to talk. often there were alternate explanations for my symptoms that seemed plausible. i certainly had no idea that all of my symptoms were part of an autism spectrum package.

my focus was on the goal. it didn't matter that i might have to use different methods. what mattered was reaching the goal. suppose that you are walking downtown. your goal is to get to the bank. but on your way you encounter a construction zone with a hole 20 feet long, directly in your path. you zig to the left, or zag to the right, go around the problem and keep progressing toward your goal. you probably don't stand there contemplating why it is that you can't jump

20 feet. you simply adjust, and keep moving toward your goal. that's what i did. and that worked... for awhile... [sigh]

at the beginning of elementary school, the neurotypical kids didn't seem so radically different from me. but as we got older, they exercised their ability to process non verbal cues. they developed into compliance with social norms that i wasn't aware of, or didn't understand - or didn't care about. integrating into these social norms made the neurotypical kids more functional in groups, but it also made them less genuine. they abandoned childlike qualities that are still very much a part of me. kids that i had known for years, who had been so wonderfully genuine, changed. they became less transparent, less trustworthy, less kind... and more functional in advanced social activities that i was becoming less and less able to participate in. as this divide grew, so did my awareness of my symptoms.

i also increasingly realized that i didn't want to be like the other kids. the feeling was mutual. i couldn't keep pace with their development. in some ways, i didn't even want to. as they normally developed they gained a lot, but the price seemed too high to me. their *genuine* birthright was exchanged for a *social* mess of pottage. it is heartbreaking to see a genuine person turn into something else. it feels like witnessing a type of death. it is a profound sense of loss. i think it is precisely what mr. wilson was singing about in "caroline, no". ~

the stepford kids

as the neurotypical kids developed socially, they became more concerned with reputation than character. it was more important to them to be thought of as nice than it was to actually *be* nice. that made no sense to me. it still doesn't. do you want a business partner who just has a reputation for honesty, or would you rather have a partner who actually *is* honest? do you want your colonoscopy performed by someone who just has a reputation for competence, or would you rather have someone who actually *is* competent?

as we entered our teenage years, two differing perspectives became more defined. many of the normal kids viewed me as someone who almost couldn't *function*. i viewed many of the normal kids as people who almost couldn't *think*. both views were alarmingly accurate.

the more i observed the differences between myself and the NT kids, the more i didn't want to be anything like them. if i had been diagnosed and sent to a therapist, especially back then, it might not have worked out very well. if i had perceived therapy as an attempt to make me like the other kids, i might have resisted strongly. the thought that i could be like those duplicitous social automatons would have been repugnant to me. it still is.

if there had been just one set of unwritten social rules, and if they had been applied consistently by everyone, then i might have been willing to try to accommodate them. but i didn't know that unwritten rules existed. i still might not know exactly what they are, but i do know that they change from person to person - and they are not applied consistently. i think at times they also require a certain ethical flexibility. these nuances may be natural for a neurotypical brain to process, but they represent a plethora of briar patches for my brain to navigate. i'm probably not capable of fully learning something that complex, and i am certainly not willing. ~

middle school shock

for most of elementary school, i had a consistency that was beneficial to me. for two semesters each school year i would have the same teacher, the same classmates and the same classroom. that familiar consistency gave me a foundation from which i could figure out how to function in the group. that changed when i entered junior high school in seventh grade.

in addition to a new school, i had a plurality of teachers and classrooms. that semester is a blur to me. it was also the time when the social development of the neurotypical kids left me in the dust. my peers were no longer interested in old pastimes like richie rich comic books and pink panther cartoons. their personalities became more complex and less transparent. even though i had known them for years, they became unrecognizable to me in their behaviors. they didn't seem like the same familiar people anymore. we were part of the same world, but we were worlds apart. ~

madman across the middle school

RJ was one of many neighborhood kids that i had known for years. in seventh grade, he decided that it was time for him to have a favorite singer - *just like all the other kids*. he had to choose carefully. if he picked the wrong one, then the other kids might not approve. he asked me if i thought elton john might be a good choice. i didn't know what to say. i didn't understand that type of "thinking". i'm not sure i even consider that to *be* actual thinking. but RJ was smart. he wouldn't have thought like that back in first grade. it took the social cesspool of seventh grade to pull that nugget out of his... uhhh... brain.

my favorite singer at that time was johnny cash. i didn't know of anyone else in the entire school who liked johnny cash, but it didn't occur to me to care about that. many people like what they know, but i know what i like. RJ picked elton john as his favorite singer, not because he liked the music, but because he thought that would be acceptable to junior high school kids in 1975... ~

visual learning and memorization

i once knew a young aspie who had difficulty understanding fractions. he didn't understand why 1/6 was less than 1/3, because he reasoned that 6 was a bigger number than 3. he needed a way to make the concept interesting and visual. with candy bars and a knife he quickly understood fractions, because he would rather have 1/3 of a candy bar than 1/6 of a candy bar. problem solved.

throughout most of elementary school i didn't know left and right. i had a visual memory in my head that i used every time i needed to distinguish left and right. i remembered when i was learning to shoot a basketball. my dad indicated that i had missed a shot to the left, and i needed to shoot more to the right. that mental image was a device that i used for years.

when i was in sixth grade, i won the school spelling bee. there was no doubt that i was going to win it. our study books were filled with words that the contest list would be chosen from. it was a very large number of words, but it was a finite number. so i memorized every word. every single one. not the definitions - just the spellings. i might not have known what "unorthodox" meant, but i could spell it. ~

3
general strategies

since elementary school, i have used 3 general strategies. the first one i used much more when i was younger. the third one became much more prominent as i got older. but i have always used all three. they are:

1. find a way to do it.
2. find a way to look like i can do it.
3. find a way to live without it.

sometimes i have to use an alternate method that my brain will let me do. in school i was unable to do "the new math", so i got the answer by doing it the old way. i could visualize it in my head without physically writing it out, and i could get the correct answer. so the teacher was unaware that i was faking the process. that example combined the first two strategies. the third strategy is very evident in my solitary adult life. just ask anyone who knows me well. if you can *find* anyone that knows me well. ~

self accommodation

i am always puzzled when a kid is in therapy, but he doesn't know that he's on the autism spectrum - or what that means. that seems almost as strange as going to a cancer doctor, but never being told that you have cancer. i think aspie kids should be equipped with the knowledge of what their symptoms are, and how they manifest. one reason i had so much anxiety is because i didn't understand what was happening. with such knowledge, i could have made my own accommodations in a more sophisticated way. i can do that now, but it would have done me much more good earlier in life. many of my failures were situations where i never had any chance of success. i wasted a lot of time and effort, because i didn't fully understand my symptoms. ~

developmentally accelerated

the best way to motivate an aspie might be through one of his interests. parents often do this in the form of simple bribery. "if you learn this and do that, then i'll buy you the video game you want". but it can be more sophisticated, with opportunities to learn useful concepts and skills. aspies have seemingly endless enthusiasm for their interests, and that can be a good thing. it's much easier for a parent to channel a child's enthusiasm than it is to try and create enthusiasm where none exists.

suppose the child is an obsessive pokémon collector. the parent could buy him a lawn mower, and money earned from mowing neighborhood lawns could be spent on his hobby. he might earn enough to buy gold plated pokémon paraphernalia from japan off ebay. that will get his attention. he could learn that he's capable of financing his interests himself. he could learn monetary concepts, as he has to budget for gasoline and mower maintenance. he could learn social skills, as he maintains and expands his customer base. while his socially adept classmates are standing around talking to each other, this kid can have his own business already.

keep in mind how smart these aspie kids are. it might occur to him that instead of mowing a $30 lawn himself, he can pay his socially adept classmate $20 to do it for him... while he pockets the extra $10. how's that for turning the tables on "developmentally delayed"?

i might chuckle when someone says that i'm "developmentally delayed". it's a true statement... but they say it as if they're not! hal i primarily think of myself as developmentally alternative. i reject the notion that developmental delay only applies to select types of people. everyone is delayed in some way. some NTs live their entire lives without developing the ability to think independently. some NTs never develop beyond the emotional level of a child. that is colossal developmental delay. they just don't know it, and they certainly don't want it pointed out to them by someone like me. ~

the danish gambit

even people who have some knowledge about autism spectrum disorders can make the mistake of assuming that only one symptom is at play in a given situation. it is almost always more complex than that. in chess the issue might not be about what a single piece is doing. more often the issue is about what multiple pieces are doing. in much the same way, life on the autism spectrum is intricate.

some people assume that the reason i rarely go to a movie theater is because of the crowd of people. that's *one* reason. but there are plenty of other reasons, including some that you might not think of. because of my sensory issues, i don't wear socks and shoes for two hours unless i have to. because of my peculiar brain, i am sometimes unable to process a movie plot in real time. if i watch a dvd at home, then i have the luxury of replaying a scene that i had difficulty understanding. i can pause the disc for a moment, and let my brain catch up with what i just saw. sometimes i have to watch a movie three or four times before i can keep up with all the plot twists, quick action and special effects. ~

the negativity loop

sometimes symptoms and characteristics reinforce themselves as they interact. if i'm socially inept and i lack a marketable skill, then i will probably have a low income. that makes it less likely that i can afford to be married, which can make me even more socially unconventional. any symptom or characteristic can become part of a more complex equation. if that interaction creates an endless loop, things can get extreme.

atypical eating can lead to obesity, which can lead to being socially withdrawn, which can lead to sitting on the couch while eating massive quantities of junk food. a negativity loop like that is how some people end up being grotesquely overweight. calories are our friends.

breaking the cycle of a negativity loop can be especially difficult for some aspies. i am a creature of habit, and that is not going to change. the best i can hope for is to possibly replace a troublesome habit with a less troublesome one. but it might be like an AA function where everyone is guzzling caffeine and inhaling nicotine, as they congratulate each other on being drug-free. there may not be any perfect solutions, but perhaps there are workable ones. ~

complexity and competing factors

decisions that are mundane and simple for NTs can be more complex for me. suppose someone wants me to go to a restaurant. i have to consider many factors that might agitate my brain. what kind of traffic will i have to drive through to get there? will i be stuck in a cramped booth? will i be sitting under bright fluorescent lights? will it be busy and noisy? will i be sitting at a table with 3 other people, who will all be sending me non verbal cues that my brain can't process? and what else do i have to do that day, that i have to keep my brain functional for?

if i have that much drama in my thoughts over the prospect of eating chicken fingers, then it isn't surprising that marriage, parenthood and career are impossibly herculean concepts to me. i look at those things in much the same way that i look at space travel. it's impressive, but it's nothing i'm ever going to do. does high functioning autism make me a low functioning person? it sure does, at least in the neurotypical world. those who insist that my disorder does not define me should try living with it for a few decades, before making such a bold proclamation.

there are many things i have to consider, but often those factors are in opposition to each other. i think that NTs might experience this when they make important decisions like buying a car. they might like a big vehicle with plenty of room, but then the fuel economy won't be as good. they might like leather seats and a fancy stereo, but then it will cost more. they might covet a sporty coupe, but then there won't be room for cargo. they will have to consider various competing factors, and determine the best cross section of features that works for them. i have to analyze many smaller aspects of life in that same way. my deliberation must seem like ridiculous overthinking to NTs - and for them it would be - but for me it's necessary. ~

"i know you can do that"

sometimes people confidently assert that i'm capable of doing something - and sometimes they are technically correct. at least in the short term. but they don't understand that i won't be able to sustain it. i can speak to a class of occupational therapy students for an hour, but that doesn't mean i can be a public speaker all day, everyday. my brain would get overwhelmed.

i have to consider the cost of what i choose to do. let me give you a physical example to illustrate the point. NTs can choose to jump off the roof, but they usually don't because they know that the painful consequences might be too severe. NTs understand an external, physical example like that. but comprehending an autism spectrum disorder can be elusive for them, because it isn't their experience. they can assume their basic functionality in the neurotypical world, and build on that foundation to successfully pursue more complex, timely accomplishments. but for me basic functionality *is* the accomplishment.

an autism spectrum brain can be like an old computer that doesn't have enough RAM to run multiple, complex applications. if i try to do too much, my brain will freeze up - and i will have to retreat and reboot. that is why some aspies have better days and worse days. if you catch me on a day when my brain isn't too taxed, i might seem higher functioning. on another day when my grey matter is a-splatter, i might seem... ahem... lower functioning.

it is commonly estimated that a significant majority of aspies do not work full-time. i can balance life much better when i'm just working part-time. i'm at my best when i'm not working at all. during periods when i do work, i have to save money and live simply to prepare for the inevitable extended vacation that i will need. there have been many occasions when i have taken significant time off from working, and lived off of savings. i sure could use one of those sabbaticals right now. but there are competing factors for me to consider. i like getting paychecks. i like buying toys. i like having health insurance. so i keep working as long as i reasonably can. i have to keep constricting other areas of my life to carve out enough brain functionality to keep working. i stretch that rubber band as far as i can, but when it finally breaks i have to take time off. ~

lowered expectations

my favorite way to get a job is for someone else to initially get hired. when the first choice doesn't work out, sometimes an employer will call me back - rather than undergo a whole new search and interview process. at that point they're just hoping to fill the position quickly, with someone who will be marginally okay. that's a standard i can meet! on a scale of 1 to 10, i am perhaps an 8 as an employee. if employers expect me to be a 9, then they will be disappointed. but if they think i'm a 7, then they'll be pleased when they realize that i'm an 8. if they think i'm a 6, then they'll be ecstatic when they realize that i'm an 8. this strategy has worked very well for me. ~

avoiding the cookie cutter

i have to be careful about what type of job i choose to work. some work environments essentially require employees to be neurotypical. i cannot fit into that cookie cutter. it's pointless to try. attempting to be a cashier, who has to smile and look customers in the eye, is not ideal. with bright fluorescent lights and a busy atmosphere, it might be a bad idea.

i prefer to work night shifts with lower light, less people and less noise. working night shifts can also be an excellent excuse for not attending social functions during the day, when i need to sleep. a job like overnight security can be a fairly good fit. it tends to be solitary, dark and slow paced, with a lot of routine. such employers highly value dependability and consistency. i tend to work jobs like that. they usually have three main requirements: the ability to pass a drug test, the ability to pass a background check, and... a pulse.

armed with that trio of credentials, i've found that i can usually get a job. the number of people who cannot pass a drug test and a background check is staggering. i was once hired for a security job without an interview. they explained that out of several dozen applications, i was the only person that passed the background check. another employer asked me if i was in the witness protection program, because he had never seen a background check come back so fast.

the ability to work a job and live independently continues to be one of my main concerns. but as i close in on reaching my senior discount status, i'm hopeful that i'll find a way to remain marginally employable. like a football team that is ahead in the fourth quarter, i don't have to make a big score - i just have to run out the clock. ~

to reveal or not to reveal

my opinion is that it is better to inform an employer about having an autism spectrum disorder. one reason is that i'm unwilling to try to keep track of who gets to know and who doesn't. that's too much work. it's easier if everyone knows. another reason is that employers and coworkers might be more willing to make reasonable accommodations, if they understand that i have a disorder. but the main reason i advocate transparency is because people will sense that i'm different. if they don't understand what that difference is, then they might fabricate an explanation that is more problematic than the actual truth. then they might gossip, which can cause the fallacy to grow. sadly, i know about this all too well.

at one job i was suddenly fired. i tried to get my employer to tell me why, but he wouldn't. i later found out that someone had been stealing money, and the gossip had focused on me. my employer and coworkers suspected me, because they didn't have a context for understanding the differences that they perceived about me. i was an easy target. some time later the employer caught the person who was stealing from him. when i found out who it was, i wasn't surprised - but the damage had already been done to me. i had lost my job, because i had been the victim of gossip.

at another job something of value went missing, and a supervisor had a "gut feeling" that i was to blame. another person defended me, because she knew how out of character that would be for me. the person who spoke up for me had known me for about twenty years, but my accuser didn't know me well. she just sensed that i was different, and therefore suspect. but if the second person hadn't known me for so long, that might have been enough for scuttlebutt to spread. once gossip gains momentum, some people will be like a dog with a bone, refusing to let it go - even if the gossip is proven to be false. it can be as if they lose the ability to think rationally. this herd mentality can be breathtakingly misinformed. i've seen it up close, and i know whereof i speak.

if you take 100 individuals who all have an IQ of 115, and put them together to comprise a social group, the "group IQ" might seem more like 85. the process of the herd mentality can occur with tremendous speed. gossip and suspicion become conviction. conviction becomes disdain and excommunication. these building blocks of ignorance have a momentum that i cannot stop. that's why i am extremely reluctant to put myself in a position where i have to rely on a group of people. the larger the group is, the lower the chance that rational thinking can prevail.

as a marginalized outsider, i see the underbelly of group dynamics in a way that most people will never fully understand. some people are just trying to make sense out of what they perceive. others seem to think that they're performing a public service, by weeding out an undesirable element - as if my oddities were contagious - as if i might be breathing up all their valuable air. but if they understand the truth about why their aspie coworker is so different, it might help in avoiding misunderstandings. the developmental delay of not maturing beyond gossip is common among NTs. my hope is that perhaps the truth can be salacious enough for them. maybe they can just gossip about the truth. ~

to speak or not to speak

in my experience, it is often true that some neurotypical people in the workplace do not like to be corrected - regardless of how wrong they are, regardless of the severity of negative consequences that their error will cause. they particularly do not like to be corrected by someone that they view as being intellectually inferior. they hate that. it chafes at them like cactus underwear.

that suggests an obvious strategy of not saying anything. maybe i should just keep my head down and stay out of the line of fire, eh? sometimes that works. but that might lead to another problem. if i know that consequences will be incurred and i don't offer a word of warning, then that will make me partially responsible. so the challenge is how to carefully, tactfully say enough to avoid responsibility - but not say enough to make anyone mad. hmmm... that's a fine line, and it sometimes isn't possible. even when it is possible, it requires an innate social sense and a calibrated subtlety that many aspies are not good at. it may also require an ethical compromise that i'm not willing to make.

i had a job where my employer did something dishonest. he was trying to appease a coworker who was a bully. people with high functioning autism know well that appeasement does not work with bullies. we've been natural targets since elementary school. we understand that if the bully gets his way, that will only reinforce the unsavory behavior. i spoke up about it with my employer in private. it was a delicate situation. he knew that i was the only one who was aware of his dishonesty. i warned him about the consequences that were going to happen, and he got mad and fired me. some time later the consequences i warned him about happened, culminating with the bully physically attacking the employer's girlfriend. after that the employer asked me to return to work, and i did.

NTs might navigate a situation like that without the roller coaster ride of being fired and rehired, and they might do so out of necessity. most people live paycheck to paycheck. they can't afford sudden unemployment. but i would rather be blameless than employed. sometimes taking a stand is a duty. the consequences i incur in that process are part of that duty. ~

to think, or not to think

as if i had a choice, heh heh. it's part of my nature to have thoughts that would not be well received by others. that is why some aspies are almost mute, unless they're around people they trust. of course, there are other aspies who bloviate incessantly. achieving a happy medium can take time and effort.

i often have curious thoughts that would not be appropriate to express in certain circumstances. i'll give you an example that i'm not proud of. but it's a glimpse into how some of us on the autism spectrum think sometimes. i was working in a health care facility one night when a patient died. it was expected. she was elderly. the husband was heartbroken. the staff looked at him, and perhaps their first thought was how sad it was that this man had just lost the love of his life. that was the *fourth* thought that occurred to me.

my first thought was that the timing of her death would make my paperwork easier. my second thought was that we would soon have a room available to accept another patient. my third thought was that the body wouldn't be removed until after midnight, so they would get billed for another day. all three of those thoughts were true and practical, but none of those thoughts would have been appropriate to express to the grieving husband. if you think the thoughts an aspie verbalizes aren't appropriate, then just imagine the content of the thoughts that aren't expressed. ~

the difficult coworker

in my experience, workplace environments tend to have one person, and usually only one person, who is very unpleasant to be around. these people can be male, but in my experience they are most often female. these people have so much in common with each other that i will construct a composite example. let's call her "gertrude".

gertrude is workplace poison personified. she is fundamentally miserable. she is smart, but not nearly as smart as she thinks she is. she does not understand the difference between intelligence and wisdom. she is not in charge, but she thinks she should be. she does not understand that the only thing limiting her potential is herself. she thinks the best way to elevate herself is by stepping on someone else. she is very quick to make an accusation, especially if it is uninformed. her baseline is to be rude, unsympathetic and unkind. she is capable of better behavior for short periods, but that requires much effort and she cannot sustain it. she has a very high opinion of herself, but she doesn't seem to realize that nobody else shares that view. she seems personally offended that anyone else might have an ounce of joy in their life. sadly, ten good employees aren't enough to make up for the damage that just one "gertrude" can do.

gertrude is a symptom of a deeper problem. the underlying problem is that someone in authority is letting that cancer grow in the workplace. such dereliction at the top of the organization will manifest in other issues. it's an indication that i might want to keep my employment options open.

sometimes coworkers ask me how i put up with gertrude. i have developed a perspective that has been helpful to me. i sometimes share it with coworkers who want to strangle gertrude, and it seems to help them also. we have to be around gertrude part of the time, but she has to *be* her 24 hours a day. she has the worst part of that deal, by far. so i don't have to respond with anger. gertrude has my pity, which is perhaps the last response she would ever want from anyone. ~

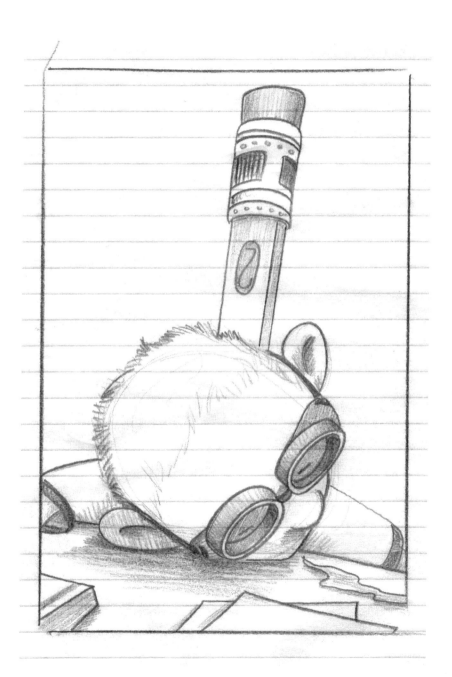

Bewildered employers

i have a long list of former employers. many of them ask me to
come back to work. some of them keep asking for years. they don't
understand why i left, they don't understand why i resisted working
increased hours, they don't understand why i was unwilling to accept
a promotion... and they don't understand why they weren't able to
entice me with money. often i would be content with a lowly part-
time position, but they would want more from me than i was willing to
give. they wanted more from me than i would be able to sustain. they
thought that intelligence was equivalent to capability.

sometimes i left because i perceived that their ethics were amiss, but
mostly i left because my time was up. sometimes i need a break. a
chance to move the stress meter down closer to zero for awhile. in
any job, there is usually some key aspect of my duties that i'm not
capable of doing. however i might be capable of faking it for awhile.
i always wanted to leave before they found out how compromised my
brain was.

over the years, i got better at sometimes being able to mitigate
the anxiety that could plague me. but even if i keep the stress
from manifesting into anxiety, there is another issue. that stress will
eventually turn into the physical breakdown of my body. i can
persevere for awhile, but not indefinitely. when i attempt too much
in the neurotypical world, i am going against the grain of my nature.
there will be consequences. ~

running on empty

what if your car had a very small tank that could only hold one gallon of gasoline? that would affect the way you drive. you would always be fearful of running out of fuel. attempting long trips would be very difficult. even short trips might require careful planning.

when it comes to social dynamics and sensory issues, i have a "one gallon brain". this limited amount of functionality in the neurotypical world is a constant concern. it's a reality that i have to accommodate, because the consequences can be debilitating. i have a heightened awareness of consequences, because i am so often the recipient of them.

yet there are other ways in which i have a "twenty gallon brain". coworkers frequently ask me how i can tolerate doing a boring, monotonous job in a dark room. it would drive them crazy. i can't do some of the things that most people can do. most people can't do some of the things that i am capable of doing. ~

living independently

living on my own and being financially independent is important to me, but it applies a constant pressure that takes a toll. with strong support and encouragement from my family, i eventually got to a point where i could work, drive a car, own property and pay the bills. i kept trying, because it was expected of me. i kept trying, because i didn't know the full extent of how unsuitable i was for the task. perhaps it was also in my nature to keep trying. i kept trying and eventually i marginally got there, but i may not be able to sustain it - and i'm not sure it was worth it.

i think my lot in life was to live in my mom's basement, ride a bicycle and maybe have a newspaper route. i also think it might have been a better path for my life to take. living independently requires so much of my brain functionality that there is little left for other important aspects of life. when i try to do too much, i run the risk of just continuing to exist - rather than living vibrantly.

i'm not in a hurry to die, but in some ways i am ready. i want the struggle to be over. i want my tapestry of failure to end. and yet i have an undeniable survival instinct. sometimes i feel like a walking contradiction. ~

the appeal of the nuclear option

when people have something chronic, something that can't be fixed, something that can't be reasoned with... it beats them down - year after year - decade after decade. they become ready to not be alive anymore. it seems easier than living.

at first they thought of that empty darkness, and they were scared. then they looked into that empty darkness, and they saw their own reflection. eventually the thought of that empty darkness became oddly comforting. i understand that attraction. ~

emotional equilibrium

i have an experientially refined survival sense. i understand that my basic functionality is a narrowly achieved thing. sometimes my ability to work a job and drive a car exists by the slimmest of margins. i tend to maintain a cut and run mentality. if a relationship, activity, job or location is causing anxiety, or brain overload, i might excise that situation from my life - whatever it is. my emotional distance is not just a strategy for functionality. it is also a way to keep important relationships from becoming acute, which could lead to harsh choices. ~

economics

because i have always operated on a limited budget, it can be very difficult for me to spend money. i've become more willing to spend money in recent years, but those who know me would still characterize me as frugal.

as i get older, i have noticed that i am not immune to the inverse relationship between time and money. when people are young they have more time, and they are willing to spend it to get money, or save money. when people are older they have more money, and they're willing to spend it in order to get time, or save time. if there is a thrifty expenditure that will improve my quality of life, i sometimes try to do it without overthinking it. that's a fairly recent development for me. it's easy for me to overthink a relatively small financial decision.

i refer to this reluctance to spend even small amounts of money as "cognitive mathematical fiscal paralysis". here's how it works. suppose i want a fast food breakfast biscuit. that tasty treat will only cost me about two dollars. i can afford that. i should be able to spend two dollars without deliberation. but then i think about how much that would be if i did it everyday. that would be $700 a year! suddenly my breakfast biscuit seems opulent and i decide against the purchase, at least until i have a coupon...

i can be very patient about waiting to buy something until i can get the very best deal. i wanted a star trek movie on dvd, and after a period of years i finally did get it. i waited until i found a used one for $1. there are thousands of examples like that across my lifetime. those cumulative savings add up to a lot of lucre.

my parents did me a favor by not giving me an allowance as a kid. it forced me to make the best use of the money i would get on my birthday and at christmas. that prepared me for adult life on a limited budget. i remember long ago, when the price of candy bars went up to ten cents. there was one store that had a lot of stock at the old price of five cents. i would ride my bike for miles to save five cents per candy bar. frugal, eh? it gets worse. there was no sales tax on purchases under 25 cents, so i only bought a few at a time. but eventually that store raised the price to ten cents, like all the other stores had done. that was a sad day.

the iPad that this book was typed on didn't cost me any money. my employer will sometimes offer Target gift cards as incentive to work an extra shift. i earned gift cards until i had enough to march into the store and purchase my iPad with them. that was a good day. ~

3,
2,
1,
zero!

3 iPods
2 macbooks
1 iPad
0 girlfriends

Bike Boy

the bicycle is one of the best human inventions ever. there is
something wonderful and mystical about self-powered locomotion.
it's a more profound bio-mechanical connection to the vehicle
than operating a car. it makes sense and it feels right. as a kid,
the bicycle expanded the horizon for my need to observe. in life
i'm not much of a participant, but i can be quite the observer. my
bicycle gave me the ability to go anywhere i wanted. it was the one
physically coordinated activity that i could do well. if i tried to fit in
socially my effort wouldn't yield much, but with my bike the amount of
effort i put into it translated into real accomplishment. best of all, it
could be a solo activity. i could ride all over town, see all kinds of
stuff and still be alone with my thoughts.

riding a bike is my superpower. i seem to be the only person who can
ride a bike all day long and still get fatter. it doesn't make sense,
because i ride my bike everywhere. i ride it to the ice cream store, to
the donut store, to the candy store... - it's a mystery... ~

internal combustion

i did not own a car until my mid twenties. i relied on my bicycle
for transportation longer than most teenagers do. i had driving
education in high school, additional driving lessons after that, and i
drove some on a learning permit with a parent at my side. but i didn't
get a license until about the age of nineteen. my first motor vehicle
was a 50cc motorcycle. it was not a big step up from a bicycle. it
was small, light and not too powerful. it was exactly what i needed to
start driving regularly. some time later, i got a 200cc motorcycle. it
took time to work up to the size and expense of a car.

bicycle skills translate quite well to operating a motorcycle. balance,
braking, turning and shifting on a bicycle are similar enough to riding
a motorcycle. it doesn't seem like such a huge leap. motorcycle skills
can apply to operating a car. shifting on a motorcycle isn't vastly
different to a manual transmission in a car. the clutch, the gas control
and the shifter are in different places, but the concepts are alike.

the size of a car intimidated me. it still does. it helped me to be able
to acclimate to busy traffic and increased speed without the added
burden of driving something big. i prefer small cars, assuming i can
fit my bulbous body in them. traffic, parking spaces and garages are
much easier for me with a smaller car.

when i drive, i have to keep a significant following distance that will
allow me more reaction time. if the car in front of me brakes suddenly,
then i might need an extra second to respond, because my brain
might not instantly process what is happening. in congested city
traffic or interstate traffic, i sometimes have to pull over and let my
brain rest for awhile. i frequently use the same routes, and it can be
very difficult for me to break that routine, even when i need to. if i
need to deviate from my normal route, i'll have to recite the alternate
turn out loud over and over as i approach it. even then i might not
remember to make the alternate turn.

surprisingly, years of playing video games helped me with aspects of learning to drive. they required me to develop the ability to be aware of multiple moving objects at various speeds on different trajectories. i might be limited to a bicycle if not for the pac-man school of driving.

driving can be a tough nut to crack for some aspies. i once knew an aspie who eventually married, had kids and worked full-time. but he was always generally agitated - and he didn't drive. he wouldn't even consider becoming a driver. it seems that aspies can figure out how to successfully do some of life's ubiquitous activities, but perhaps not all. ~

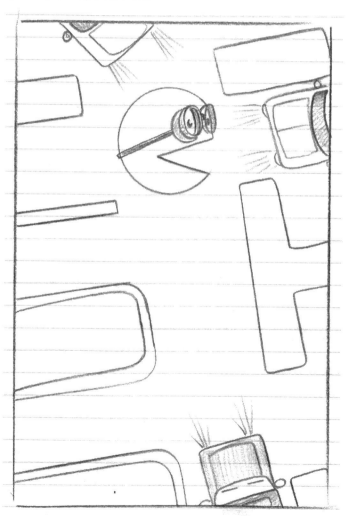

creating my own comfort zone

as much as i can, i try to create my own world that is comfortable for me. when i was young, it was my room with my comic books, music and toys - and my activities that i enjoyed and could do by myself, like riding a bike. now it's my condo, with my iPad and my guitar - and my activities that i enjoy and can do by myself, like riding a bike or a motorcycle. are you noticing a pattern?

when i do have to navigate the neurotypical world, i am sometimes very introspective and observant. there is a sense in which i am alone with my thoughts, even when i'm in a crowded room. i am always interested in maintaining familiarity, and assessing unfamiliarity. that's why i am often looking around in different directions. i'm looking for anything familiar that will make me feel more comfortable. i'm also scanning for unfamiliarity. unfamiliarity can equal danger. when i get home, i can let my guard down. when i'm out in the neurotypical world, i feel like the prey at the watering hole. when i'm alone at home, i'm safer in the tall grass. ~

rain man

as an adult i saw the "rain man" movie, and i also saw real savants
on a tv show. i noticed some familiar behaviors. i started to
get the idea that whatever it was that was different about my
brain... might be related to savantism. many years later, i saw a
documentary about a savant named kim peek. again, i noticed some
uncomfortably familiar behaviors. one day, at age 47, i was chatting
with a relative who was an occupational therapist. i mentioned the
kim peek documentary to her, and i volunteered some information that
i had never fully shared before. i told her that i had something like
savantism, but not as extreme. she looked down and thought about
what she was going to say.

she knew what i was talking about, because of her education and
experience. she had known about me for a long time, but she
was stunned to hear me say it. as i prodded her for information,
i became aware of the terms "asperger's syndrome" and "autism
spectrum disorder". that conversation was also the first time i ever
heard anything about non verbal cues. non verbals had been the
huge missing piece of the puzzle to me. i had wondered how other
people could spot me so quickly - like when the herd knows that one
is wounded. sometimes i would enter a room and be shunned before
i had even said anything. non verbals were the "secret handshake"
of socializing that i never knew about.

knowing the terminology allowed me to look up relevant information
on the internet. i realized that i must be on the autism spectrum.
it just fit. it gave me a context for understanding things in my
experience that i previously couldn't make sense of. i knew that

there would be some resistance to the idea from members of my family, so i figured that a diagnosis from a neurologist could serve as an independent authority. i also thought it might be helpful to my family if they understood the reasons for my peculiar behaviors and my emotional distance. having a diagnosis was new, but the behaviors were not new to them.

my family always knew that i was smart. they would say that there was nothing wrong with me, but they would also look out for me because they knew that there was some kind of issue. they had that unresolved dichotomy in their thinking. if there was something i couldn't do, they sometimes thought it was because i wasn't trying. they didn't know how hard i had to try in order to do almost anything substantive. i didn't want them to know, and i was clever at hiding the full extent of my issues.

because of my auditory issues and other symptoms, i had a vague fear that i might be institutionalized if the extent of my difficulties became known. i didn't think of myself as authentically human. such thoughts would come and go, depending on how well i was doing. i developed the mindset of an imposter. over time, i increasingly dismissed the idea that i might ever function well. i just had to find ways to marginally function. i just had to find ways to survive.

i never wanted anyone to know the level of difficulty that i had. now everyone knows. life is simpler that way. i'm different, and i can't hide that fact from anybody. i could try to hide the specific nature of what that difference is, but some people would still know my exact issues. i don't have a choice about being on the autism spectrum. the only choice i have is if i'm going to hide it or embrace it. ~

the ephemeral nature of close friendships

i generally do not have the skills, time, will or energy to maintain friendships. it is also difficult for me to trust anyone enough to think of them as a friend. i tend to view things in black & white terms. nuanced grey areas can be slippery for my brain to grasp. i don't know how to trust in a measured way. people are either worthy of my trust or they are not. i tend to think that the vast majority are not. but it was not always so.

i think two things have changed in this regard since the days of my youth. one is that i'm more aware now, but the other is that society is less trustworthy now. it used to be that i could give everyone the benefit of the doubt, and i would only occasionally be disappointed. but now, to protect myself, i have to assume the worst about everyone, and only occasionally will i be pleasantly surprised. there used to be a sense of shame about misbehavior. now it's more like a sense of revelry, even entitlement.

but suppose a trustworthy person does somehow run the gauntlet of my odd personality, and becomes my friend. for me to maintain a rapport, i have to see that person regularly, and that can only last for awhile. people have to be who they are wired to be. neurotypical people have to be the social butterflies that they are. they have to meet the time consuming demands of marriage, family, career and social groups. they can't indefinitely spend all their time hanging out with me in a cave. nor should they try to. that's not me being preemptive. it's reality. ~

frankly, scarlett...

i am frequently unwilling to do things that i think are fundamentally stupid. some things truly are inherently stupid. other things may just be unsuitable for me, because i'm such an odd duck. there are many aspects of life that i don't have the energy for. i have a noticeably finite amount of functionality. i will not waste that scant resource on things that don't matter to me.

i marvel at people who do daily tasks that seem like a waste of time to me. they make their bed. they tie their shoes. if i concerned myself with things like that, i'd never get anything important done. i wear slip on shoes, or i tie shoes loosely so they can function as slip on shoes. i don't understand why i would make my bed, because i'm just going to mess it up again later. i do not exist to serve the bed. the bed exists to serve me. my limited functionality needs to be spent on important things, like working a job and driving a car. those things make it possible for me to live independently, which is much more important to me than having shoes that look stylish. ~

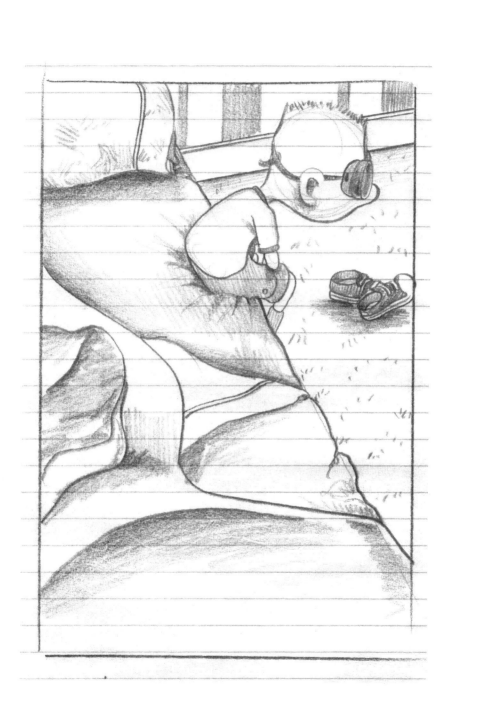

the other side
of the coin

for obvious reasons, i'm better at one to one social interaction than i am with group interaction. but my symptoms are just one side of that coin. let me shed some light on the other side.

NTs are diverse. some NTs are quite impressive. but many NTs are only at their best when they are not in a group. a *person* is smart, but *people* can seem less smart. sometimes when an NT is apart from the group, his IQ seems to rise 30 points in some ways. when they are not in a group, many NTs are more capable of rational, independent thought. they may find it easier to be honest, when they're not in a group. they may be more comfortable behaving as genuine individuals, when they're not in a group.

it is that honest, intelligent, more genuine version of the person that i am comfortable being around. but, like moths to the flame, NTs spend much of their lives being part of the group. to varying degrees, they quickly pivot back into being compromised versions of themselves. they benefit greatly from being high functioning members of the group, but the cost is that it can make them severely low functioning as individuals. ~

pants on fire

some people have a strong aversion to telling the truth. being untruthful can become very natural for some of them. they might even lie when the truth would serve their purposes better. it's as if they no longer know the difference between lying and truth-telling. that is problematic for me, because i am so dependent on verbal communication. when i can't trust what a person says, i might limit my exposure to them. i might decide to avoid them completely. ~

keen perception

practitioners and family members sometimes notice that certain people are unable to establish a rapport with individuals on the autism spectrum. i know of one good reason for that. i can't fully explain it, but i'm very aware of it - and i can describe it.

i have a finely honed ability to detect counterfeits, and some people set that alarm off big-time. it may not have anything to do with the words that they say. it's as if i can see a variance between their outward appearance and their internal essence. they may disguise themselves with highly developed social skills, but i don't process those cues well. that may be why i have uncluttered insight to see deeper than the social veneer. often i know precisely what it is that i'm noticing in their behavior, but there is a specific type of occurrence that i almost never talk about.

sometimes i see someone who is particularly spurious, but he is skilled enough to deceive most people. he may present himself well, but he is a predator. i see right through his facade, and he knows it. this perception can occur quickly, it can happen without verbalization - and it is never wrong. i may see someone across a room, and somehow i will discern his subterfuge. in that uncomfortable moment, we will be very aware of each other. it's not exactly like i can see into his soul. it's more like i can see an empty vacuum where his soul should be. i can't explain the process. i don't know *what* it is, but i certainly know *that* it is. ~

Being Blunt

i'm reluctant to mince words regarding things that are important to me. i think the world is in desperate need of more blunt truth, not less. things should be properly labeled and ideas should be clearly stated. suppose your child is about to touch a hot stove. will you remain silent, because you're worried about offending him? will you tell him that touching the burner will make the oven spit out candy? i don't think so. you'll tell him the blunt truth. anything else would be a disservice, because there are consequences. to say anything other than the truth would actually be quite rude.

of all my peculiar behaviors, the number one thing i do that makes people mad... is that i tell the truth. some people are deeply offended that i respect them enough to not lie to them. i agree that it's a problem, but i do not agree that it's *my* problem.

when someone is offended by the truth, i generally don't care. i'm not denying that perhaps i should care. i'm just admitting that i really don't care. it's not because i dislike the person. it's not because i'm mean. it's just practical. it's too trivial to register on my radar. if i chose to spend all my time and energy worrying about not offending people, i might get good at it - but it would be the only thing i could do. it wouldn't be a life worth living. besides, some people need to be offended. if a deadbeat dad is offended at the notion that he should man up to his responsibilities... then let him be offended. i really don't care. the axiom is instructive: either you will stand for something, or you will fall for anything.

there are some people who are fundamentally conflict-oriented. their lives seem to be defined by who they are mad at. i've noticed that this bizarre trait seems to run in families. some people are so cursed in this way that they make *me* feel normal by comparison! that's quite a feat. i have observed that if people want to be offended, then that is exactly what they will be. if people want to get mad, then that is exactly what they will do. regardless of anything i do, or don't do. i cannot make their decisions for them. i am not the catalyst. their character is the catalyst. especially regarding important things, i would rather be correct than popular. frankly, when i associate with quality individuals... it isn't a problem. that's one reason why some aspies are very selective about who they spend time with. if you don't make the cut, it isn't necessarily a reflection on you... but it might be. ~

the sphincter principle

sometimes people are perplexed with me, because of my odd characteristics and behaviors. my brain doesn't process non verbal cues well, and i may not express the non verbals that they consider to be appropriate. people respond to this confusion in various ways. some react with patience, some with instruction, some with amusement, some with curiosity, some with frustration... and some with anger. the manner in which people choose to behave reveals their character.

when someone chooses to behave like a kind, patient and wise person... it's because he actually *is* a kind, patient and wise person. when someone chooses to behave like an ass... it is NOT because i'm on the autism spectrum. it's because he *is* an ass. i don't get to choose what kind of brain i have, but he does get to choose if he's going to be an ass - and he has made the wrong choice.

to kind people, some aspies might like to say "thank you". to unkind people, some aspies might like to say "*thank* you... and the horse you rode in on". ~

jekyll and hyde

some people seem to embody two distinct personalities. one that is nice, and one that is not. i've never understood how these people can be kind and generous, but then quickly change to being mean and hateful. my need for consistency makes me very uncomfortable around such people. i never know which version of the person i'm going to get. that uncertainty is very taxing on my brain.

i've had ample opportunity to observe these people. the ones that i have known have been overwhelmingly male. they have all had their issues exascerbated at times by alcohol use, and most of them increasingly succumbed to their darkness as they got older. behavior that started in their youth as passionate zest for life and rapscallionesque charm... got out of hand somewhere along the way. eventually, most of their admirable qualities and their sense of joy became extinguished. their souls seemed to die years before their bodies did. ~

the unforgivable crime of having a pulse

some people are so invested in their delusions... that they are offended by the very existence of people like me. they have fooled themselves into thinking that all of their behaviors and abilities are superior. but reality has a way of bursting that bubble. they cannot comprehend how a clumsy, socially dense aspie can be better than them at *anything*. it seems so incongruous to them. everything might be copacetic, as long as they can view me as being completely inferior - but reality forces them to eventually figure out that there is a gigantic hole in their philosophy... and that can infuriate them.

these situations are further complicated by built in communication barriers. the way i think is so different. my strengths are in such different areas. decades ago, i was surprised when someone got mad and loudly said to me "you think you're better than me". i replied "at *what?*". i was confused by his statement, and he was flabbergasted by my reply. as he stood there dumbfounded, i became even more confused. how did my two-word reply render him speechless? it was as if we had been speaking different languages. ~

the thing about self esteem

some people have a low opinion of me. other people have a high opinion of me. neither reputation is entirely deserved. my self esteem is not very dependent on the opinions of other people. common notions about low self esteem and high self esteem don't make sense to me. the salient issue is whether a person has *accurate* self esteem, and that can be a function of one's character. if a person of low character also has low self esteem, then that is very appropriate. ~

the thing about name-calling

i have a long held understanding that when people engage in hateful name-calling, they are revealing their character. they unintentionally say more about themselves than whatever they are trying to sully me with. they expose themselves as being the type of people who behave like that. they are not happy. they have curiously chosen to be miserable. it is far more soul-crushing to *be* a person who does that, than it is to simply be the recipient of such hatred. like the child who insists on touching the hot stove, the consequential punishment is built in to the activity. when a person chooses to be unsavory, he willfully takes the diamond of his soul and turns it right back into coal. ~

the thing about bullying

bullies choose to be brutal, and that may be the only language they understand. in school there were glorious occasions when a scrappy little kid who was being bullied... eventually decided to hit the bully back. he'd hit him hard. he'd hit him in the face. he'd hit him repeatedly, and he wouldn't stop hitting the bully until he was pulled off and restrained.

all who beheld this viscerally wondrous sight knew that it was justified and appropriate. it is satisfying to know that a bully will eventually get his humiliating comeuppance. it's also the best thing for the bully. without an attitude adjustment, the bully may never develop into a worthwhile person. ~

a tale of two densities

sometimes people would be annoyed with me, because of how dense i could be in some areas. this often led to name-calling. the most common term i heard was "retard". when a person called me that, he was like a modern day caiaphas. i actually do think of myself as being *socially* retarded. that's one of the terms i would use to describe myself before i knew what my disorder was. the other thing i would say was that i was like an idiot-savant... only without the savant part. people would laugh, but i was only half-joking. those were the best ways i could think of to describe myself. i also used to describe my brain as being like a street system, where some roads were always under construction.

so if some people were frustrated with me because they thought i was stupid, imagine how perturbed they were when it would become apparent that, in some ways, i was more skilled than they were. they hated that. when someone insisted that i was a moron, but then he couldn't beat me at chess... that could greatly annoy him. some people never could reconcile my juxtaposition of intelligence and denseness.

i had more awareness about the ways in which they were dense, and they had more awareness about the ways in which i was dense. but they were in the majority, so my denseness was a disorder... and their denseness was *normal*. in what ways were they dense? keep reading, if you dare. ~

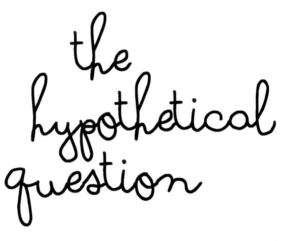

the hypothetical question

people who ask the question already know what my answer will be. what they really want to know is *why*, and that is something that some aspies only discuss in hushed tones, amongst each other. the question: "if there was a *cure* for asperger's, would you want to become neurotypical?". many aspies answer this question with a resolute "no", as do i. why is that? let me give you the polite answer first.

i would not choose to become neurotypical, because being on the autism spectrum is all i know. it is part of my identity. for me to cease being on the autism spectrum would be to cease being me. it gives me a type of insight i would not want to give up. it gives me a deep appreciation for some things that are important to me.

that's the polite answer. it has the added benefit of being true. but it pussyfoots around the real issue. imagine for a moment that the reverse question was asked of an NT. "if there was a *cure* for being an NT, would you choose to be on the autism spectrum if you could?". i think most would answer "no" - and they might state it in polite terms. but what would they really be thinking? they would be horrified to think that they could be like me. i feel that same apprehension at the thought of being neurotypical. i'm not sure how much value there is in explaining exactly why, because many aspies already know it, and many NTs might not want to know it. but here it is.

many people with high functioning autism, who have lived in the neurotypical world for a long time, have observed that most NTs are more messed up than we are - but developmental delay occurs in other areas for NTs. it may be convenient for the majority to decide that their characteristics are entirely positive, but it is unrealistic. many neurotypical people are prone to unwarranted emotional responses, that are not the result of sound thinking. most neurotypical people have a stunning lack of discernment. they are often susceptible to a type of group-think and gossip that can be jaw-droppingly ignorant. to an aspie mind, it can seem a lot like willful stupidity. these NT traits can be very obvious and discomforting to aspies, just like aspie traits can be obvious and discomforting to NTs. many aspies have the audacity to believe that we have the better package, even though our difficulties may be considerable.

many people tend to think that if something is "normal", then that means it is better. but if something is "normal", then it is not exceptional. it's normal to fly coach, but it's exceptional to fly first class. i reject the notion that what is normal is therefore to be preferred. it's normal for a toddler to wet his pants, but that doesn't mean it's a wonderful thing. i may not intend something desirous when i use the terms "neurotypical" and "normal". i may think something is suspect because it is "normal".

there may be a sense in which we all do what we are wired to do. NTs tend to place a higher premium on communal functionality, because they are socially adept. aspies tend to place a higher premium on independent thinking, because we are analytically adept.

NTs understand that there is functionality and approval in the herd. aspies understand that sometimes the herd is being corralled toward the slaughterhouse. aspies know that the herd is capable of stampeding at any moment, and we will be the ones who get trampled. one might also observe that if you're in the middle of the herd, the only view you have is the rear end of the cow in front of you - and anywhere you step there might be a steaming pile waiting for you. ~

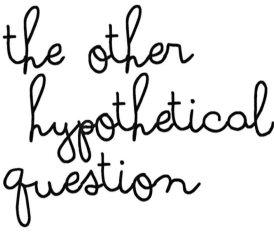

the other hypothetical question

what would my life be like now, if i had been born with a neurotypical brain? i can only guess, based on people i know who are roughly my age. if i wasn't an aspie, i would be able to multitask and successfully engage in a wider variety of life experiences. i would be physically coordinated enough to participate in activities like team sports and dancing. i would be an accomplished career person, able to navigate "office politics". i would live in a very nice house and drive very nice cars. i would have expensive toys like boats and recreational vehicles.

i would rarely get to use those toys because i would be working long hours at a job i hate, in order to pay for them. i would have a high income, but i would rarely have any money in my pocket. i would be deep in debt with credit card interest and mortgage payments. i would have several unruly children of various parentage. i would be stuck with my third wife, because another divorce would bankrupt me. i would have many "friends", few of whom i could actually count on. i would fit in and go with the flow of trendy, vapid ideas - but there might be a gargantuan discrepancy between the image i project, and the reality of my soul.

do i really know people who fit that description? yes, i do. i suspect you do also. ~

are aspies smarter than nts?

it's not necessarily about intelligence. it's about how intelligence manifests in different ways. i'm reasonably smart, but my intelligence doesn't flex its muscles in the area of social interaction. NTs are much more proficient at using their intelligence to maneuver in a social context. my intelligence is more active in my ability to be discerning, and my tendency to think independently. i am far less likely to fall prey to emotionalism. my understanding is that emotions are valid when they are in response to meaningful truth. that is in stark contrast to the common practice of being emotional for the sake of being emotional. ~

meds

i'm suspicious of anti-anxiety medications and antidepressants. i feel like i should be able to deal with issues by ordering my life accordingly. i admit that has involved choices that NTs might not understand. but if i'm having an issue, then that may be an indication that i need to change what i'm doing.

i'll give a physical example to illustrate the point. if i'm burning my hand on a hot stove, i need to change my behavior. i don't need to dope myself up so that i can continue to leave my hand there, and cause more damage. i understand that view is too simplistic to fit every situation and every person, but perhaps it should be the first thing to try. i don't view my peculiarities as negatively as other people do, so i'm reluctant to medicate them. frankly, i have to put up with far more poppycock from some normal people than they have to put up with from me. perhaps they need to take a pill more than i do. ~

what about therapy now?

i think the therapist / aspie relationship might be similar to a doctor / patient relationship. it's more likely to work well when each party understands that the other has unique expertise. that's why i don't like going to a doctor. i understand that the practitioner has clinical expertise. but i have the experiential expertise of knowing my specific body. so i need just the right doctor to have a good experience. i assume i would also need just the right therapist to have a worthwhile experience.

sometimes clinicians have a cookie cutter mentality, and i have never been able to fit myself into anyone's cookie cutter. with varying degrees of sophistication, i have been contemplating my issues for several decades. if there's an expert on my specific experience... it isn't the therapist. i'm not an expert on the subject of autism, but i am *the* expert on my experience of living with it.

i think my behaviors are largely set in stone by now. they are so automatic for me that i don't think i could change them much. at this point, i'm more like a fish that needs to stay in the water as much as possible. i stay in my comfort zone as much as i can. i have no doubt that a skilled therapist could teach me some useful things, but i would never really "speak the language". it would be like visiting mexico with a spanish-english dictionary. it could be marginally helpful, but i still wouldn't "fit in". in some ways i don't even want to fit in. it would be a mistake to try. ~

square peg, round hole

the ability to "fit in" is not in my skill set. i am not capable of turning
off my divergently analytical brain - and i wouldn't be willing to, even
if i could. fitting in would require compromises that are abhorrent
to me. like a star fleet officer who wouldn't want to become a borg
drone, i would rather be dead than mindlessly compliant. even if my
resistance is futile, i cannot deny my individualistic nature. ~

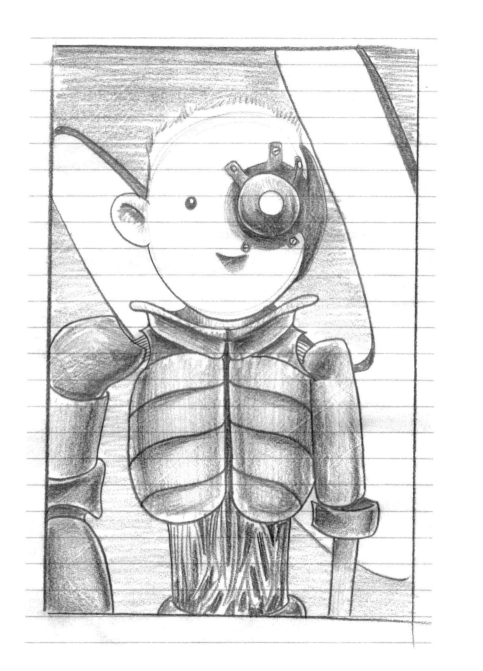

the maytag repairman

sometimes people tell me that they think i am lonely. there is some veracity to that observation, but they say it as if being lonely is a bad thing. i am not distressed by solitude - i embrace it. over the years i've found that there is a comfortable predictability about being alone. others may see it as a curse that has engulfed me, but i have always tended to view it more as a goal to be achieved. i have spent much effort in the pursuit and preservation of a solitary lifestyle.

the more lonely i am, the less i have to deal with my social challenges. the more lonely i am, the less i have to endure the behavior of other people, *especially some people* - their lies, their gossip, their tantrums and their arrogant ignorance are things that i would rather avoid. i don't want to be bombarded with those behaviors, and i certainly don't want to fit in with them. ~

a note for occupational therapy students

it is important to understand that academic knowledge may not be complete. academic preparation is a foundation for a deeper understanding that can be developed as a practitioner. when you treat people with autism, it may be an opportunity to learn from them as they learn from you. when you meet a mom who lives with an autistic child 24 hours a day, she knows salient information that wasn't in your textbook. combining that experiential knowledge with academic knowledge can be formidable. academic knowledge can set the ball up on the tee, but experiential knowledge can hit the ball out of the park. ~

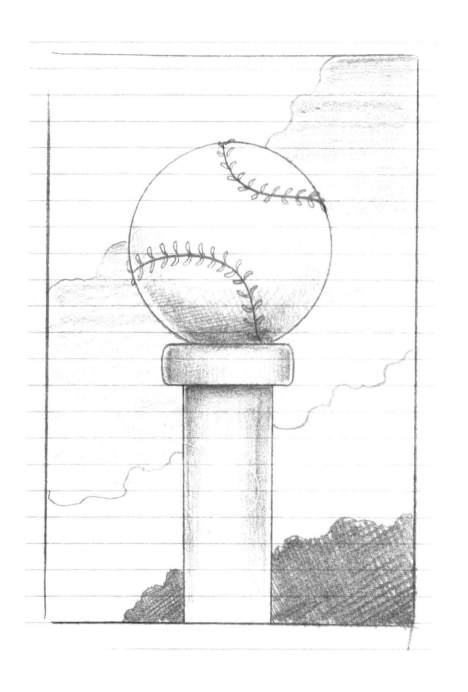

autistic alchemy

my blend of symptoms, characteristics, strategies and abilities is always changing. it isn't simple and consolidated, where everything gets worse or everything gets better. sometimes i can improve my baseline. when i was young, my brain would overload if i rode a bicycle at 20 mph, but i can do it now. sometimes my baseline takes a nosedive. my ability to memorize information is now greatly reduced, and any ability i ever had to multitask is now almost nonexistent. but while some of my issues get worse, i may be able to compensate by becoming more sophisticated in my strategies. i also benefit from becoming wiser over time. it's a very complex package, and it's always changing. ~

not easily

life is so hard.
learning is so hard.
multitasking is so hard.
social activities are so hard.
will these things ever get better?

hardly. ~

diversity

my life as an incorrigible aspie has been somewhat middling, but there are other people on the autism spectrum who function quite well. some are aspies, some have classic autism, some get therapy, some don't get therapy, some are very aware of their symptoms and some are not so aware. but most of those who do well probably have two things in common. the first is a support structure of family or friends. the second is that they are allowed to pursue their interests, and be who they are. i suggest that parents and practitioners start with those two things as the foundation of their efforts.

my characteristics put some people at *dis*-ease, but i do not have a disease. maybe i don't need to be medicated. maybe i don't need to be fixed. maybe i am the way that i am supposed to be. ~

134

post script

choices have consequences.

in the interim between the writing of this book and its publication, sobering events have occurred involving perpetrators who were thought to have had asperger's syndrome. one of those events happened where i live - in casper, wyoming.

choices have consequences.

aspies sometimes develop customized philosophies that provide a framework for making sense of the world; prisms through which they view everything else. these prisms vary from person to person: math & science, religion, political ideology, conspiracy theories, extreme devotion to an interest, etc. - but some people seem to also choose a specific or generalized contempt for humanity.

choices have consequences.

if i had made certain choices at certain times, it's possible that i could have ended up as a misanthropic monster. having a moral firewall is what kept me from such a fate. morality is immutable. individual opinions of right and wrong vary from person to person, legality varies from place to place and generation to generation, parental examples vary from household to household - but true morality does not change. aspies are like everyone else in this regard. if one doesn't adhere to an independent, authentic, authoritative, immutable source of morality, then it is possible that one might end up on a very evil path.

choices have consequences.

For more information on C. G. Meloy please visit

www.lifeandspectrum.com

CPSIA information can be obtained at www.ICGtesting.com
Printed in the USA
LVOW10s2302080916

503853LV00016B/228/P